Hippocrene
CHILDREN'S
ILLUSTRATED
RUSSIAN
DICTIONARY

ENGLISH - RUSSIAN
RUSSIAN - ENGLISH

Compiled and translated by the Editors of Hippocrene Books

Interior illustrations by S. Grant (24, 81, 88); J. Gress (page 10, 21, 24, 37, 46, 54, 59, 65, 72, 75, 77);
K. Migliorelli (page 13, 14, 18, 19, 20, 21, 22, 25, 31, 32, 37, 39, 40, 46, 47, 66, 71, 75, 76, 82, 86, 87);
B. Swidzinska (page 9, 11, 12, 13, 14, 16, 23, 27, 28, 30, 32, 33, 35, 37, 38, 41, 42, 45, 46, 47, 48, 49, 50,
52, 53, 56, 57, 58, 59, 60, 61, 62, 63, 66, 68, 69, 70, 71, 72, 73, 75, 77, 78, 79, 83), N. Zhukov (page 8, 13,
14, 17, 18, 23, 27, 29, 33, 34, 39, 40, 41, 52, 64, 65, 71, 72, 73, 78, 84, 86, 88).

Design, prepress, and production: Graafiset International, Inc.

Hippocrene Children's Illustrated Russian Dictionary
Copyright © 1999 by Hippocrene Books, Inc.
Fourth printing, paperback edition, 2008.

Cataloging-in-Publication Data available from the Library of Congress.

ISBN-13: 978- 0-7818-0892-7
ISBN-10: 0-7818-0892-8

Printed in China.

For information, address:
Hippocrene Books, Inc.
171 Madison Avenue
New York, NY 10016
www.hippocrenebooks.com

INTRODUCTION

With their absorbent minds, infinite curiosities and excellent memories, children have enormous capacities to master many languages. All they need is exposure and encouragement.

The easiest way to learn a foreign language is to simulate the same natural method by which a child learns English. The natural technique is built on the concept that language is representational of concrete objects and ideas. The use of pictures and words are the natural way for children to begin to acquire a new language.

The concept of this Illustrated Dictionary is to allow children to build vocabulary and initial competency naturally. Looking at the pictorial content of the Dictionary and saying and matching the words in connection to the drawings gives children the opportunity to discover the foreign language and thus, a new way to communicate.

The drawings in the Dictionary are designed to capture children's imaginations and make the learning process interesting and entertaining, as children return to a word and picture repeatedly until they begin to recognize it.

The beautiful images and clear presentation make this dictionary a wonderful tool for unlocking your child's multilingual potential.

Deborah Dumont, M.A., M.Ed.,
Child Psychologist and Educational Consultant

РУССКИЙ АЛФАВИТ

RUSSIAN ALPHABET

Аа	Кк	Хх
Бб	Лл	Цц
Вв	Мм	Чч
Гг	Нн	Шш
Дд	Оо	Щщ
Ее	Пп	Ъъ
Ёё	Рр	Ыы
Жж	Сс	Ьь
Зз	Тт	Зз
Ии	Уу	Юю
Йй	Фф	Яя

RUSSIAN PRONUNCIATION

Letters	Pronunciation system used	
а	a	as in 'father' but short
а	aa	as in 'car' (long)
ай	oy	like *ye* in 'bye'
г	g	as in 'garden'
е	ye	as in 'yes' (at the beginning of a word)
ё	yo	as in 'yolk' (at the beginning of a word)
ей	ey	as in 'hey'
ж	zh	like the *s* in 'leisure'
з	z	as in 'zebra'
и	i	as in 'eel' but short
	ee	as in 'see' when long
й	y	as in 'kayak'
о	o	as in 'omit' when short
	oh	as in 'door' when long
р	r	as in 'burro' (trilled as in Spanish)
с	s	as in 'salt'
у	oo	as in 'tooth'
х	kh	like the *ch* in Scottish 'loch'
ц	ts	as in 'cats'
ч	ch	as in 'cherry'
ш	sh	as in 'ship'
щ	shch	as in 'fresh cheese'
ь	”	at the end of a syllable softens the preceding consonant
ы	y	like the *i* in 'big'
э	eh	like the *e* in 'elbow'
ю	yu	like the *you* in 'youth'
я	ya	as in 'yard'

ъ at the end of a syllable: short pause, as between words

(i) softens the preceding consonant: press the tongue to the palate while pronouncing the consonant, for example sa-mo-l(i)ot.

' Apostrophe before a syllable indicates that this syllable is stressed

airplane самолёт
sa-mo-'l(i)ot

alligator аллигатор
al-l(i)i-'ga-tor

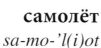

alphabet алфавит
al-fa-'vit

antelope антилопа
an-ti-'lo-pa

antlers оленьи рога
o-l(i)'en"-ee ro-'ga

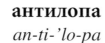

apple   **яблоко**
'yab-lo-ko

aquarium   **аквариум**
ak-'va-r(i)i-oom

arch   **арка**
'ar-ka

arrow   **стрела**
str(i)e-'la

autumn   **осень**
'o-s(i)en''

baby младенец
mla-'d(i)e-n(i)ets

backpack рюкзак
r(i)uk-'zak

badger барсук
bar-'sook

baker пекарь
'p(i)e-kar"

ball мяч
m(i)ach

balloon воздушный шар
voz-'doosh-ny shar

banana банан
ba-'nan

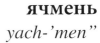

barley ячмень
yach-'men"

barrel бочка
'boch-ka

basket корзинка
kor-'z(i)i-nka

bat летучая мышь
l(i)e-'too-cha-ya mysh

beach пляж
pl(i)azh

bear   медведь
m(i)ed-'v(i)ed"

beaver   бобр
bo-'br

bed   кровать
kro-'vat"

bee   пчела
pche-'la

beetle   жук
zhook

bell   колокол
'ko-lo-kol

belt   пояс
'po-yas

bench   скамья
skam-'ya

bicycle   велосипед
v(i)e-lo-si-'p(i)ed

binoculars   бинокль
bi-'nokl"

bird   птица
'pti-tsa

birdcage   птичья клетка
'pt(i)i-chya 'kl(i)et-ka

black   чёрный
'chyor-ny

blocks   кубики
'koo-bi-ki

blossom   цвет
tsv(i)et

blue   синий
'see-n(i)y

boat   лодка
'lod-ka

bone   кость
kost''

book книга
'kn(i)i-ga

boot сапог
sa-'pog

bottle бутылка
boo-'tyl-ka

bowl миска
'm(i)is-ka

boy мальчик
'mal"-chik

bracelet браслет
bras-'l(i)et

branch ветка
'v(i)et-ka

bread хлеб
khl(i)eb

breakfast завтрак
'zav-trak

bridge мост
most

broom метла
m(i)et-'la

brother брат
braat

brown   коричневый
ko-'rich-n(i)e-vy

brush   щётка
'shchyot-ka

bucket   ведро
v(i)ed-'ro

bulletin board доска объявлений
dos-'ka   'ob'-yav-l(i)e-n(i)y

bumblebee   шмель
shm(i)el"

butterfly   бабочка
'ba-boch-ka

cab   такси
tak-'s(i)i

cabbage   капуста
ka-'poos-ta

cactus   кактус
'kak-toos

café   кафэ
ka-'feh

cake   торт
tort

camel   верблюд
v(i)er-'bl(i)ood

camera   **фотоаппарат**
fo-to-ap-pa-'rat

candle   **свечка**
'sv(i)ech-ka

candy   **конфета**
kon-'f(i)e-ta

canoe   **байдарка**
bay-'dar-ka

cap   **шапка**
'shap-ka

captain   **капитан**
ka-p(i)i-'tan

car   автомобиль
af-to-mo-'bil"

card   карта
'kaar-ta

carpet   ковер
ko-'v(i)or

carrot   морковь
mor-'kov"

(to) carry   нести
n(i)es-t(i)i

castle   замок
'zaa-mok

cat   кошка
'kosh-ka

cave   пещера
p(i)esh-'che-ra

chair   стул
stool

cheese   сыр
syr

cherry   черешня
che-'r(i)esh-nya

chimney   труба
troo-'ba

chocolate   шоколад
sho-ko'lad

Christmas tree   ёлка
'yol-ka

circus   цирк
tsyrk

(to) climb   лазить
'laa-zit"

cloud   облако
'ob-la-ko

clown   клоун
'klo-oon

coach карета
ka-'r(i)e-ta

coat пальто
pal"-'to

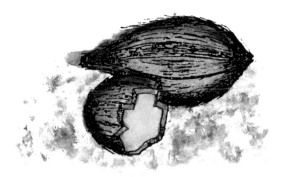

coconut кокос
ko-'kos

comb расчёска
ras-'chyos-ka

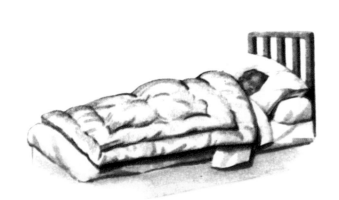

comforter одеяло
o-d(i)e-'ya-lo

compass компас
'kom-pas

(to) cook варить
va-'rit"

cork пробка
'prob-ka

corn кукуруза
koo-koo-'roo-za

cow корова
ko-'ro-va

cracker печенье
pe'che-nye

cradle колыбель
ko-ly-'bel"

(to) crawl   ползать
'pol-zat"

(to) cross   переходить
p(i)e-r(i)e-kho-'d(i)it"

crown   корона
ko-'ro-na

(to) cry   плакать
'pla-kat"

cucumber   огурец
ogoo-'r(i)ets

curtain   занавеска
za-na-'v(i)es-ka

(to) dance   танцевать
tan-tse-'vat"

dandelion   одуванчик
o-doo-'van-chik

date   число
'chis-'lo

deer   олень
o-'len"

desert   пустыня
poos-'ty-n(i)a

desk   парта
'par-ta

dirty   грязный
'gr(i)az-nyy

dog   **собака**
                                             so-'ba-ka

doghouse   **конура**   **doll**   **кукла**
                 ko-noo-'ra   *'kook-la*

dollhouse   **игрушечный домик**   **dolphin**   **дельфин**
                  ig-'roo-shech-ny 'do-mik   *'del"-fin*

donkey   **осёл**   **dragon**   **дракон**
               o-'s(i)ol   *dra-'kon*

dragonfly   стрекоза
str(i)e-ko-'za

(to) draw   рисовать
ri-so-'vat"

dress   платье
'plat"-ye

(to) drink   пить
pit"

drum   барабан
ba-ra-'ban

duck   утка
'oot-ka

eagle　　　орёл
o-'ryol

(to) eat　　　есть
yest"

egg　　　яйцо
yay-'tso

eggplant　　　баклажан
ba-kla-'zhan

eight　　　восемь
'vo-sem"

elbow　　　локоть
'lo-kot"

elephant　　　слон
slon

empty   пустой
poos-'toy

engine   паровоз
pa-ro-'voz

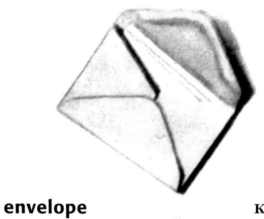

envelope   конверт
kon-'v(i)ert

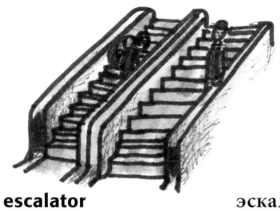

escalator   эскалатор
es-ka-'la-tor

Eskimo   эскимос
ehs-ki-'mos

(to) explore   исследовать
is-'sl(i)e-do-vat"

eye   глаз
glaz

face   лицо
l(i)i-'tso

fan   вентилятор
ven-t(i)i-'l(i)a-tor

father   отец
o-'t(i)ets

fear   страх
strakh

feather   перо
p(i)e-'ro

(to) feed   кормить
kor-'m(i)it"

fence забор
za-'bor

fern папоротник
'pa-po-rot-n(i)ik

field поле
'po-l(i)e

field mouse полевая мышь
po-l(i)e-'va-ya mysh

finger палец
'pa-l(i)ets

fir tree ель
yel"

fire огонь
o-'gon"

fish рыба
'ry-ba

(to) fish удить
oo-'d(i)it"

fist кулак
koo-'lak

five пять
'p(i)at"

flag флаг
flaag

flashlight фонарик
fo-'na-rik

(to) float держаться на поверхности
dyer'-zhatsya na po'-verkhno-sti

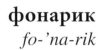

flower цветок
tsv(i)e-'tok

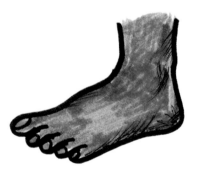

(to) fly летать
l(i)e-tat"

foot нога
no-'ga

fork вилка
'v(i)il-ka

fountain фонтан
fon-'tan

four четыре
che-'ty-r(i)e

fox лиса
l(i)i-'sa

frame рама
'ra-ma

friend друг
droog

frog лягушка
l(i)a-'goosh-ka

fruit фрукты
'frook-ty

furniture мебель
'm(i)e-bel"

garden   сад
sad

gate   ворота
vo'-ro-ta

(to) gather   собирать
so-b(i)i-rat"

geranium   герань
g(i)e-'ran"

giraffe   жираф
zhi-'raf

girl   девочка
d(i)e-voch-ka

(to) give давать
da-'vat"

glass стакан
sta-'kan

glasses очки
och-'kee

globe глобус
'glo-boos

glove перчатка
p(i)er-'chat-ka

goat коза
ko-'za

goldfish золотая рыбка
zo-lo-'ta-ya 'ryb-ka

"Good Night" "Спокойной ночи"
spo-'koy-noy 'no-chi

"Good-bye" "До свидания"
do svi-'da-n(i)ya

goose гусь
goos"

grandfather дедушка
'd(i)e-doosh-ka

grandmother бабушка
'ba-boosh-ka

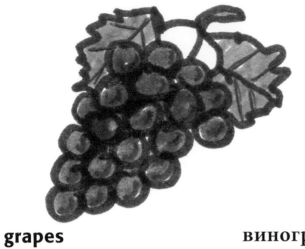

grapes
виноград
v(i)i-no-'grad

grasshopper
кузнечик
kooz-'n(i)e-chik

green
зеленый
z(i)e-'l(i)o-nyy

greenhouse
парник
par-'n(i)ik

guitar
гитара
g(i)i-'ta-ra

hammer   молоток
mo-lo-'tok

hammock   гамак
ga-'mak

hamster   хомяк
kho-'m(i)ak

hand   рука
roo-'ka

handbag   сумка
'soom-ka

handkerchief   платочек
pla-'to-chek

harvest урожай
oo-ro-'zhay

hat шляпа
'shl(i)a-pa

hay сено
's(i)e-no

headdress головной убор
go-lov-'noy oo-'bor

heart сердце
's(i)er-tse

hedgehog ёж
yozh

hen   курица
'koo-r(i)i-tsa

(to) hide   прятаться
'pr(i)a-tat''-s(i)a

highway   шоссе
shos-'seh

honey   мёд
m(i)od

horns   рога
ro-'ga

horse   конь
kon''

horseshoe   подкова
pod-'ko-va

hourglass   песочные часы
pe-'soch-ny-ye cha-'sy

house   дом
dom

(to) hug   обнимать
ob-n(i)i-'mat"

hydrant   пожарная колонка
po-'zhar-naya ko-'lon-ka

ice cream　мороженое
mo-'ro-zhe-no-ye

ice cubes　кубики льда
'koo-bi-ki l''da

ice-skating　кататься на коньках
ka-'tat-s(i)a na kon''-'kakh

instrument　инструмент
in-stroo-'m(i)ent

iris　ирис
'ee-r(i)is

iron　утюг
oo-'tyug

island　остров
'os-trov

jacket пиджак
pid-'zhaak

jam джем
dzhehm

jigsaw puzzle складная картинка
sklad-'na-ya kar-'t(i)in-ka

jockey жокей
zho-'key

juggler жонглёр
zhon-'gl(i)or

(to) jump скакать
ska-'kat"

kangaroo кенгуру
k(i)en-goo-'roo

key ключ
kl(i)ooch

kitten котёнок
ko-'t(i)o-nok

knife нож
nozh

knight рыцарь
'ry-tsar"

(to) knit вязать на спицах
v(i)a-'zat" na sp(i)i-'tsakh

knot узел
'oo-z(i)el

koala bear коала
ko-'a-la

ladder   лестница
'l(i)est-n(i)i-tsa

ladybug   божья коровка
'bozh-ya ko'rov-ka

lamb   барашек
ba-'ra-shek

lamp   лампа
'lam-pa

(to) lap   лакать
la-'kat"

laughter   смех
sm(i)ekh

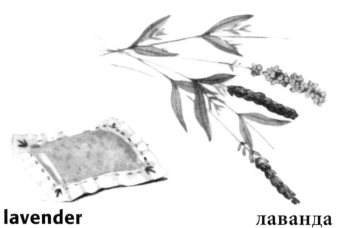

lavender лаванда
la-'van-da

lawn mower косилка
ko-'s(i)il-ka

leaf лист
l(i)ist

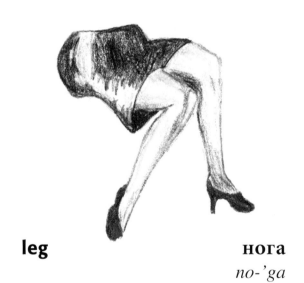

leg нога
no-'ga

lemon лимон
l(i)i-'mon

lettuce салат
sa-'lat

lightbulb   лампочка
'lam-poch-ka

lighthouse   маяк
ma-'yak

lilac   сирень
s(i)i-'ren"

lion   лев
l(i)ev

(to) listen   слушать
'sloo-shat"

lobster   омар
o-'mar

lock замок
za-'mok

lovebird канарейка
ka-na-'r(i)ey-ka

luggage багаж
ba-'gazh

lumberjack лесоруб
l(i)e-so-'roob

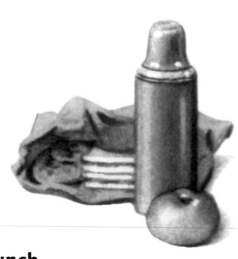

lunch обед
o-'b(i)ed

lynx рысь
rys"

magazine   журнал
zhoor-'nal

magician   фокусник
'fo-koos-nik

magnet   магнит
mag-'n(i)it

map   карта
'kar-ta

maple leaf   кленовый лист
kl(i)e-'no-vy l(i)ist

marketplace   рынок
'ry-nok

mask   маска
'mas-ka

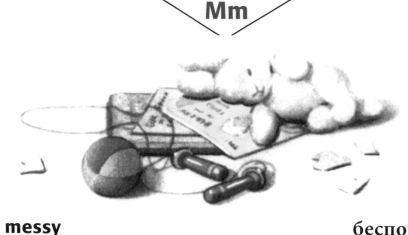

messy

беспорядок
b(i)es-po-'r(i)a-dok

milkman

молочник
mo-'loch-nik

mirror

зеркало
'z(i)er-ka-lo

mitten

рукавица
roo-ka-'v(i)i-tsa

money

деньги
'd(i)en''-gi

monkey

обезьяна
o-b(i)ez-'ya-na

moon

луна
loo-'na

mother   мать
                                  mat"

mountain   гора
                                  go-'ra

mouse   мышь
                                  mysh

mouth   рот
                                  roht

mushroom   гриб
                                  gr(i)ib

music   музыка
                                  'moo-zy-ka

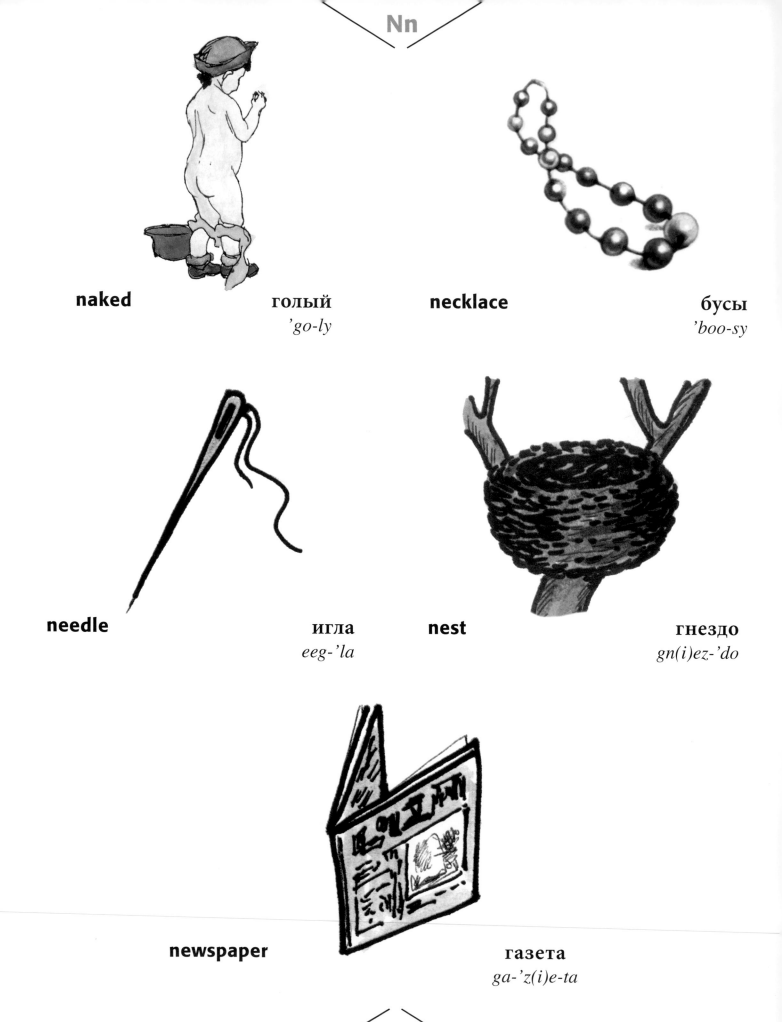

naked   голый
'go-ly

necklace   бусы
'boo-sy

needle   игла
eeg-'la

nest   гнездо
gn(i)ez-'do

newspaper   газета
ga-'z(i)e-ta

nightingale соловей
so-lo-'v(i)ey

nine девять
d(i)e-'v(i)at"

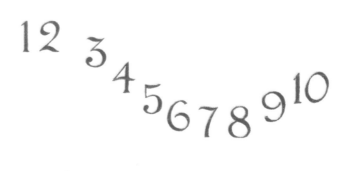

notebook тетрадь
t(i)et-'rad"

number число
ch(i)is-'lo

nut орех
o-r(i)ekh

oar весло
v(i)es-'lo

ocean liner океанский лайнер
ok(i)e-'an-sk(i)iy 'lay-ner

old старый
'sta-ry

one один
o-'d(i)in

onion лук
look

open   открыто
ot-'kry-to

orange   апельсин
a-p(i)el"-'s(i)in

ostrich   страус
'stra-oos

owl   сова
so-'va

ox   бык
byk

padlock   замок
za-'mok

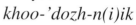

paint   краска
'kras-ka

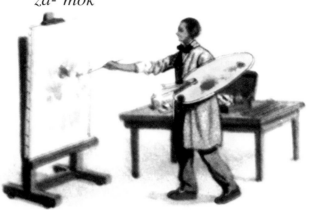

painter

художник
khoo-'dozh-n(i)ik

pajamas   пижама
p(i)i-'zha-ma

palm tree   пальма
'pal"-ma

paper   бумага
boo-'ma-ga

parachute   парашют
pa-ra-'shoot

park парк
park

parrot попугай
po-poo-'gay

passport паспорт
'pas-port

patch заплата
zap-'la-ta

path дорожка
do-'rozh-ka

peach персик
'p(i)er-s(i)ik

pear груша
'groo-sha

pebble

галька
'gal"ka

(to) peck

клевать
kl(i)e-'vat"

(to) peel

чистить
'ch(i)is-t(i)it"

pelican

пеликан
p(i)e-l(i)i-'kan

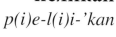

pencil

карандаш
ka-ran-'dash

penguin

пингвин
p(i)in-'gv(i)in

people

люди
'l(i)oo-d(i)i

piano   пианино
p(i)i-a-'n(i)i-no

pickle   маринованный огурец
ma-ri-no'-va-nnyy o-goo-'rets

pie   пирог
p(i)i-'rog

pig   свинья
sv(i)in"-'ya

pigeon   голубь
'go-loob"

pillow   подушка
po-'doosh-ka

pin   булавка
boo-'lav-ka

pine   сосна
sos-'na

pineapple   ананас
a-na-'nas

pit   косточка
'kos-toch-ka

pitcher   кувшин
koov-'shin

plate   тарелка
ta-'r(i)el-ka

platypus   утконос
oot-ko-'nos

(to) play   играть
ig-'rat"

plum   слива
sl(i)i-'va

polar bear   белый медведь
b(i)e-ly m(i)ed-v(i)ed"

pony   пони
'po-n(i)i

pot   кастрюля
kas'-tryu-lya

potato   картофель
kar-'to-f(i)el"

(to) pour   **наливать**
na-l(i)i-'vat"

present   **подарок**
po-'dar-ok

(to) pull   **тянуть**
t(i)a-'noot"

pumpkin   **тыква**
'tyk-va

Qq

puppy   **щенок**
shche-'nok

queen   **королева**
ko-ro-'l(i)e-va

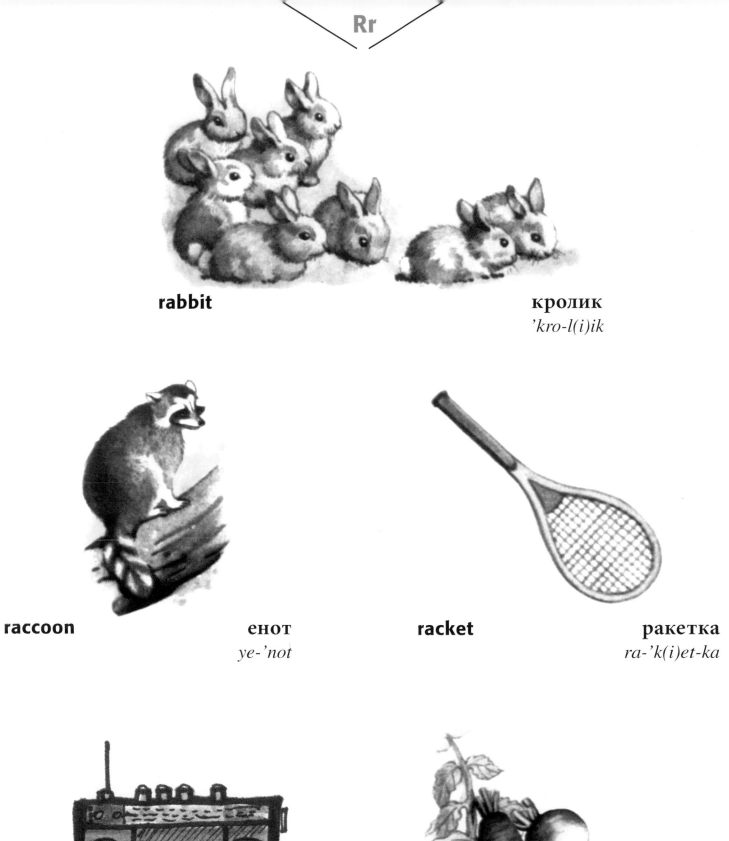

rabbit

кролик
'kro-l(i)ik

raccoon

енот
ye-'not

racket

ракетка
ra-'k(i)et-ka

radio

радио
'ra-d(i)i-o

radish

редиска
r(i)e-'d(i)is-ka

raft надувной плот
na-doov-'noy plot

rain дождь
dozhd"

rainbow радуга
'ra-doo-ga

raincoat дождевик
dozh-d(i)e-'v(i)ik

raspberry малина
ma-'l(i)i-na

(to) read　　　читать
chi-'tat"

red　　　красный
'kras-ny

refrigerator　　　холодильник
kho-lo-'d(i)l"nik

rhinoceros　　　носорог
no-so-'rog

ring　　　кольцо
kol"-'tso

(to) ring   звонить
zvo-'nit"

river   река
re-'ka

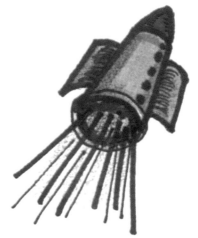

road   дорога
do-'ro-ga

rocket   ракета
ra-'k(i)e-ta

roof   крыша
'kry-sha

rooster   петух
p(i)e-'tookh

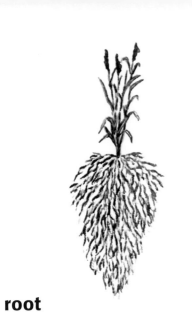

root   корень
ko'-ren"

rope   канат
ka-'nat

rose   роза
'ro-za

(to) row   грести
gres-'ti

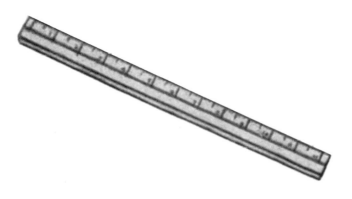

ruler   линейка
li-n(i)ey-ka

(to) run   бежать
be-'zhat"

safety pin английская булавка
an-gl(i)iy-ska-ya boo-'lav-ka

(to) sail ходить под парусом
kho-'d(i)it" pod 'paa-roo-som

sailor матрос
mat-'ros

salt соль
sol"

scarf шарф
sharf

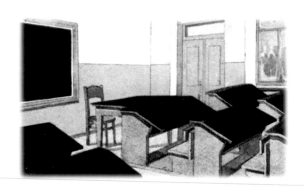

school школа
'shko-la

scissors   ножницы
'nozh-n(i)i-tsy

screwdriver   отвёртка
ot-'v(i)ort-ka

seagull   чайка
'chay-ka

seesaw   качание на доске
ka-'cha-n(i)ye na dos-'k(i)e

seven   семь
sem"

(to) sew   шить
sheet"

shark   акула
a-'koo-la

sheep   овца
ov-'tsa

shell   ракушка
ra-'koosh-ka

shepherd   пастух
pas-'tookh

ship   корабль
ko-'raabl"

shirt   рубашка
roo-'bash-ka

shoe   ботинок
bo-t(i)i-nok

shovel   лопата
lo-'paa-ta

(to) show   показывать
po-'ka-zy-vat"

shower   душ
doosh

shutter   ставень
'sta-ven"

sick   больной
bol"-'noy

sieve   сито
'see-to

(to) sing   петь
p(i)et"

(to) sit   сидеть
s(i)i-'d(i)et"

six   шесть
shest"

sled   санки
'san-ki

(to) sleep   спать
spat(i)

small   **маленький**
'ma-l(i)en"-keey

smile   **улыбка**
oo-'lyb-ka

snail   **улитка**
oo-'l(i)it-ka

snake   **змея**
zm(i)e-'ya

snow   **снег**
sn(i)eg

sock   **чулок**
choo-'lok

sofa   диван
d(i)i-'van

sparrow   воробей
vo-ro-'b(i)ey

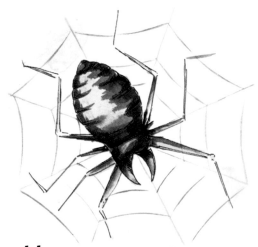

spider   паук
pa-'ook

spiderweb   паутина
pa-oo-'t(i)i-na

spoon   ложка
'lozh-ka

squirrel   белка
'bel-ka

stairs　　ступеньки
stoo-'pen"-kee

stamp　　марка
'maar-ka

starfish　　морская звезда
mor-'ska'-ya zv(i)iez-'da

stork　　аист
'aa-eest

stove　　плита
'plee-ta

strawberry　　клубника
kloob-'n(i)i-ka

subway

метро
met-'ro

sugar cube

сахар
'sa-khar

sun

солнце
sonn-tse

sunflower

подсолнух
pod-'sol-nookh

sweater

свитер
'sv(i)i-t(i)er

(to) sweep

подметать
pod-m(i)e-'tat"

swing

качели
ka-'che-l(i)i

table   стол
stohl

teapot   чайник
'chay-n(i)ik

teddy bear   мишка
'm(i)ish-ka

television   телевизор
te-le-'vi-zor

10

ten   десять
'd(i)e-s(i)at"

tent   палатка
pa-'lat-ka

theater

театр
t(i)e-'atr

thimble

напёрсток
na-'p(i)or-stok

(to) think

думать
'doo-mat"

three

три
tr(i)i

tie

галстук
'gal-stook

(to) tie

завязывать
za-'v(i)a'-zy-vat"

tiger тигр
t(i)igr

toaster тостер
'tos-ter

tomato помидор
po-mi-'dor

toucan тукан
too-'kan

towel полотенце
po-lo-'t(i)en-tse

tower башня
'bash-n(i)a

toy box   коробка для игрушек
ko-'rob-ka dl(i)a ig-'roo-shek

tracks   рельсы
'r(i)el"-sy

train station   станция
'staan-tsiya

tray   поднос
pod-'nos

tree   дерево
d(i)e-r(i)e-vo

trough   корыто
ko-'ry-to

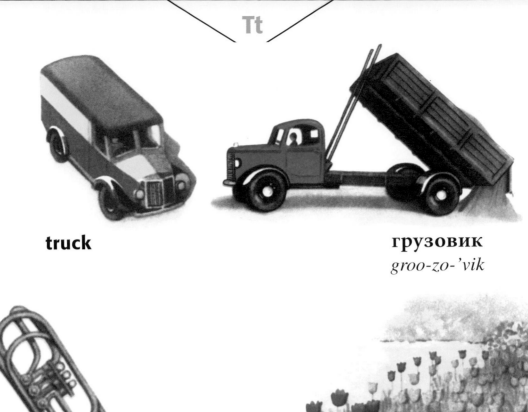

truck

грузовик
groo-zo-'vik

trumpet

труба
troo-'ba

tulip

тюльпан
t(i)ul"-'pan

tunnel

туннель
too-'nehl"

turtle

черепаха
che-r(i)e-'paa-kha

twins

близнецы
bl(i)iz-n(i)e-tsy

two

два
dva

umbrella   зонтик   **uphill**   в гору
'zontik   *v'go-roo*

Vv

vase   ваза   **veil**   вуаль
'vaa-za   *voo-'al"*

village   **деревня**
d(i)e-r(i)ev-n(i)a

violet   **фиалка**
fee-'al-ka

violin   **скрипка**
'skr(i)ip-ka

voyage   **путешествие**
poo-t(i)e-'shest-vi-ye

waiter   официант
o-fi-tsi-'aant

(to) wake up   проснуться
pro-snoot-s(i)a

walrus   морж
morzh

(to) wash   стирать
st(i)i-'rat"

watch   часы
cha-'sy

(to) watch   наблюдать
na-bl(i)u-'dat"

(to) water поливать
po-l(i)i-'vat"

waterfall водопад
vo-do-'paad

watering can лейка
'l(i)ey-ka

watermelon арбуз
ar-'booz

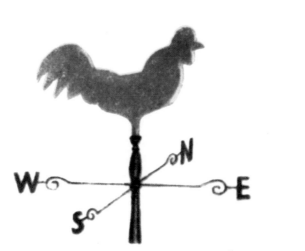

weather vane флюгер
'fl(i)oo-ger

(to) weigh взвешивать
'vz-v(i)e-shi-vat"

whale кит
keet

wheel колесо
ko-l(i)e-'soh

wheelbarrow тачка
'taach-ka

whiskers усы
'oo-sy

(to) whisper шептать
shep-'tat''

whistle свисток
svis-'tok

white   **белый**
'b(i)e-ly

wig   **парик**
paa-'r(i)ik

wind   **ветер**
v(i)e-t(i)er

window   **окно**
ok-'noh

wings   **крылья**
kryl"-'ya

winter   **зима**
z(i)i-'maa

wolf

волк
volk

wood

дрова
dro-'va

word

слово
'sloh-voh

(to) write

писать
p(i)i-'sat"

Yy

yellow　　　　　　　　　　　　　　　**желтый**
'zhol-ty

Zz

zebra　　　　　　　　　　　　　　　**зебра**
'z(i)e-braa

бусы	necklace
бутылка	bottle
бык	ox

В

в гору	uphill
ваза	vase
варить	(to) cook
ведро	bucket
велосипед	bicycle
вентилятор	fan
верблюд	camel
весло	oar
ветер	wind
ветка	branch
взвешивать	(to) weigh
вилка	fork
виноград	grapes
водопад	waterfall
воздушный шар	balloon
волк	wolf
воробей	sparrow
ворота	gate
восемь	eight
вуаль	veil
вязать на спицах	(to) knit

А

автомобиль	car
аист	stork
аквариум	aquarium
акула	shark
аллигатор	alligator
алфавит	alphabet
ананас	pineapple
английская булавка	safety pin
антилопа	antelope
апельсин	orange
арбуз	watermelon
арка	arch

Б

бабочка	butterfly
бабушка	grandmother
багаж	luggage
банан	banana
барабан	drum
барашек	lamb
барсук	badger
башня	tower
бежать	(to) run
белка	squirrel
белый	white
белый медведь	polar bear
беспорядок	messy
бинокль	binoculars
близнецы	twins
бобр	beaver
божья коровка	ladybug
больной	sick
ботинок	shoe
бочка	barrel
браслет	bracelet
брат	brother
булавка	pin
бумага	paper

Г

газета	newspaper
галстук	tie
галька	pebble
гамак	hammock
герань	geranium
гитара	guitar
глаз	eye
глобус	globe
гнездо	nest
головной убор	headdress
голубь	pigeon
голый	naked
гора	mountain

грести	(to) row
гриб	mushroom
грузовик	truck
груша	pear
грязный	dirty
гусь	goose

Д

давать	(to) give
два	two
девочка	girl
девять	nine
дедушка	grandfather
дельфин	dolphin
деньги	money
дерево	tree
деревня	village
держаться на поверхности	to float
десять	ten
джем	jam
диван	sofa
"До свидания"	"Good-bye"
дождевик	raincoat
дождь	rain
дом	house
дорога	road
дорожка	path
доска объявлений	bulletin board
дракон	dragon
дрова	wood
друг	friend
думать	(to) think
душ	shower

Е

ель	fir tree
енот	raccoon
есть	(to) eat

Ё

ёж	hedgehog
ёлка	Christmas tree

Ж

желтый	yellow
жираф	giraffe
жокей	jockey
жонглёр	juggler
жук	beetle
журнал	magazine

З

забор	fence
завтрак	breakfast
завязывать	(to) tie
замок	castle
замок	lock
замок	padlock
занавеска	curtain
заплата	patch
звонить	(to) ring
зебра	zebra
зелёный	green
зеркало	mirror
зима	winter
змея	snake
золотая рыбка	goldfish
зонтик	umbrella

И

игла	needle
играть	(to) play
игрушечный домик	dollhouse
игрушка	toy
инструмент	instrument

ирис	iris
исследовать	(to) explore

К

кактус	cactus
канарейка	lovebird
канат	rope
капитан	captain
капуста	cabbage
карандаш	pencil
карета	coach
карта	map
карта	card
картофель	potato
кастрюля	pot
кататься на коньках	ice-skating
качели	swing
кафэ	café
кенгуру	kangaroo
кит	whale
клевать	(to) peck
клоун	clown
клубника	strawberry
ключ	key
книга	book
коала	koala bear
ковёр	carpet
коза	goat
кокос	coconut
колесо	wheel
колокол	bell
колыбель	cradle
кольцо	ring
компас	compass
конверт	envelope
конура	doghouse
конфета	candy
конь	horse
корабль	ship

корень	root
коричневый	brown
корзинка	basket
кормить	(to) feed
коробка для игрушек	toy box
корова	cow
королева	queen
корона	crown
корыто	trough
косилка	lawn mower
косточка	pit
кость	bone
котёнок	kitten
кошка	cat
краска	paint
красный	red
кровать	bed
кролик	rabbit
крылья	wings
крыша	roof
кубики	blocks
кубики льда	ice cubes
кувшин	pitcher
кузнечик	grasshopper
кукла	doll
кукуруза	corn
кулак	fist
курица	hen

Л

лаванда	lavender
лазить	(to) climb
лакать	(to) lap
лампа	lamp
лампочка	lightbulb
лев	lion
лейка	watering can
лесоруб	lumberjack

музыка	music
мышь	mouse
мяч	ball

Н

наблюдать	(to) watch
надувной плот	raft
наливать	(to) pour
напёрсток	thimble
нести	(to) carry
нога	leg, foot
нож	knife
ножницы	scissors
носорог	rhinoceros

лестница	ladder
летать	(to) fly
летучая мышь	bat
лимон	lemon
линейка	ruler
лиса	fox
лист	leaf
лицо	face
лодка	boat
ложка	spoon
локоть	elbow
лопата	shovel
лук	onion
луна	moon
люди	people
лягушка	frog

М

магнит	magnet
маленький	small
малина	raspberry
мальчик	boy
маринованый огурец	pickle
марка	stamp
маска	mask
матрос	sailor
мать	mother
маяк	lighthouse
мебель	furniture
мёд	honey
медведь	bear
метла	broom
метро	subway
миска	bowl
мишка	teddy bear
младенец	baby
молоток	hammer
молочник	milkman
морж	walrus
морковь	carrot
мороженое	ice cream
морская звезда	starfish
мост	bridge

О

обед	lunch
обезьяна	monkey
облако	cloud
обнимать	(to) hug
овца	sheep
огонь	fire
огурец	cucumber
одеяло	comforter
один	one
одуванчик	dandelion
океанский лайнер	ocean liner
окно	window
олень	deer
оленьи рога	antlers
омар	lobster
орёл	eagle
орех	nut
осёл	donkey
осень	autumn
остров	island
отвёртка	screwdriver
отец	father
открыто	open
официант	waiter
очки	glasses

П

палатка	tent
палец	finger
пальма	palm tree
пальто	coat
папоротник	fern
парашют	parachute
парик	wig
парк	park
парник	greenhouse
паровоз	engine
парта	desk
паспорт	passport
пастух	shepherd
паук	spider
паутина	spiderweb
пекарь	baker
пеликан	pelican
переходить	(to) cross
перо	feather
персик	peach
перчатка	glove
песочные часы	hourglass
петух	rooster
петь	(to) sing
печенье	cracker
пещера	cave
пианино	piano
пиджак	jacket

пижама	pajamas
пингвин	penguin
пирог	pie
писать	(to) write
пить	(to) drink
плакать	(to) cry
платочек	handkerchief
платье	dress
плита	stove
пляж	beach
подарок	present
подкова	horseshoe
подметать	(to) sweep
поднос	tray
подсолнух	sunflower
подушка	pillow
пожарная колонка	hydrant
показывать	(to) show
поле	field
полевая мышь	field mouse
ползать	(to) crawl
поливать	(to) water
полотенце	towel
помидор	tomato
пони	pony
попугай	parrot
пояс	belt
пробка	cork
проснутся	(to) wake up
прятаться	(to) hide
птица	bird
пустой	empty
пустыня	desert
путешествие	voyage
пчела	bee
пять	five

Р

радио	radio
радуга	rainbow
ракета	rocket
ракетка	racket
ракушка	shell
рамка	frame
расчёска	comb
редиска	radish
река	river
рельсы	tracks
рисовать	(to) draw
рога	horns
роза	rose
рот	mouth
рубашка	shirt
рука	hand
рукавица	mitten
рыба	fish
рысь	lynx
рыцарь	knight
рынок	marketplace
рюкзак	backpack

С

сад	garden
салат	lettuce
санки	sled
сапог	boot
самолёт	airplane
сахар	sugar cube
свечка	candle
свинья	pig

свисток	whistle
свитер	sweater
семь	seven
сено	hay
сердце	heart
сидеть	(to) sit
синий	blue
сирень	lilac
сито	sieve
скакать	(to) jump
скамья	bench
складная картинка	jigsaw puzzle
скрипка	violin
слива	plum
слово	word
слон	elephant
слушать	(to) listen
смех	laughter
снег	snow
собака	dog
собирать	(to) gather
сова	owl
солнце	sun
соловей	nightingale
соль	salt
сосна	pine
спать	(to) sleep
"Спокойной ночи"	"Good night"
ставень	shutter
стакан	glass
станция	train station
старый	old
стирать	(to) wash
стол	table
стрекоза	dragonfly
страус	ostrich
страх	fear

стрела	arrow
стул	chair
ступеньки	stairs
сумка	handbag
сыр	cheese

Т

тачка	wheelbarrow
такси	cab
танцевать	(to) dance
тарелка	plate
театр	theater
телевизор	television
тетрадь	notebook
тигр	tiger
торт	cake
тостер	toaster
три	three
труба	chimney
труба	trumpet
тукан	toucan
туннель	tunnel
тыква	pumpkin
тюльпан	tulip
тянуть	(to) pull

У

удить	fish
узел	knot
улитка	snail
улыбка	smile
урожай	harvest
усы	whiskers
утка	duck
утконос	platypus
утюг	iron

Ф

фиалка	violet
флаг	flag
флюгер	weather vane
фокусник	magician
фонарик	flashlight
фонтан	fountain
фотоаппарат	camera
фрукты	fruit

Х

ходить под парусом	(to) sail
хлеб	bread
холодильник	refrigerator
хомяк	hamster
художник	painter

Ц

цвет	blossom
цветок	flower
цирк	circus

Ч

чайка	seagull
чайник	teapot
часы	watch
черепаха	turtle
черешня	cherry
чёрный	black
четыре	four
число	date
число	number
чистить	(to) peel
читать	(to) read
чулок	sock

Ш

шапка	cap
шарф	scarf
шептать	(to) whisper
шесть	six
шить	(to) sew
школа	school
шляпа	hat
шмель	bumblebee
шоколад	chocolate
шоссе	highway

Щ

щенок	puppy
щётка	brush

Э

эскалатор	escalator
эскимос	Eskimo

Я

яблоко	apple
яйцо	egg
ячмень	barley